epochs of morning light

prose poems

elena botts

Mwanaka Media and Publishing Pvt Ltd,
Chitungwiza Zimbabwe

*

Creativity, Wisdom and Beauty

Publisher:

Mmap

Mwanaka Media and Publishing Pvt Ltd

24 Svosve Road, Zengeza 1

Chitungwiza Zimbabwe

mwanaka@yahoo.com

https//mwanakamediaandpublishing.weebly.com

Distributed in and outside N. America by African Books Collective

orders@africanbookscollective.com

www.africanbookscollective.com

ISBN: 978-0-7974-8617-1

EAN: 9780797486171

DISCLAIMER

All views expressed in this publication are those of the author and do not necessarily
reflect the views of *Mmap*.

Endorsement

In poet and artist Elena Botts' new poetry collection: *epochs of morning light,* we see a shimmering, variegated new voice; we hear: "where the trees still talk to each other, and winter feels like a song..." (from When I have died we will be here).

We feel the weather of her emotions; a contract with the ethereal and the visceral, as when we stand within the short but large poem: blossoms back to under the earth: "I felt your ghost move through me out past the Baltic as though you had been in my heart the whole time." In this sensual canvas, beauty never suffers from loneliness, nor the sublime.

Each poem herein as Botts wanders memory and weaves tapestries of word worlds, reveals a true and original voice in modern poetry: allowing light to conquer darkness; darkness to defy the estate of the sun, and colors mixed in ways only an artist of the pen could fathom.

If the poems in this collection defy conventional perception, they do so with feathered prophecy and wisdom that seems anachronistic for one so young! Often, in modern poetry, pathology is glorified as if suffering is not universal in this troubled age. Botts surpasses longing and allows her reader to hike with her through urban gardens of people, and countryside, wherein their voices and after image are more than memory, but nearly a spiritual offering.

March, 2018

-Robert Milby
Hudson Valley New York poet,
Poet Laureate, Orange County, NY 2017-2019

Poems

someone left the hot water on too long. sometimes in the world it grows quiet but never so much as in my soul. there was nothing to become. you were and so was i. in the city of pigeons under the bridges the photographers are drenched in the wet and spray eyeing the under of brooklyn. i was in a fog after that first morning, watching the quiet sky blue and green and you were cold, the blanket barely about you so i tucked it in, ready to not speak to you for most of this new year your eyes are a sleep of a kind and turn different colors in the light the way you move is a message written to god and there are brief eclipsing letters all about your form and face the stories of how you decimated yourself and in surrender, rose up your eyes had closed over upon my lap and i moved gently away as though in the gaze of death but there was something beautiful about us that i could not say and in the cold morning i left.

the epochs:
i guess you could say the moon and i have been spending a lot of time together lately. recently, it has come to my attention that all my love has been in vain. i want to thank all my ghosts for being here for me. if you want to reach me i'm on the top floor of an empty building in the middle of nowhere, i also have a cell phone. or you can leave your message with mephistopheles.

and in that midnight i could not sound myself aloud and so i crept from one aching auspice to the other like a bird in a wheat field broke by the flat blue wind and wondering if this is it the plain of familiarity rolls on and on and we in it if i light my candles by the window and no one comes should i still have said those words when the universe cannot hear them the deaf ear of god as cliff face echoing i come down the mountain to sit by the train tracks and lie with my head back and my legs in the fading color of dusk waiting for a rumbling that means i'd better run as i wait i count the stars as one by one, they come out of their hidden corners burning for no one.

the earth is undone as the sky deepens into the real color first chirpings from the trees baby blue stage stream pooling holes of sky through the forest pale ochre yellow murmuring about the trees deer like stolen statues on the green fogged up bus like a ghost ship are there other people on this planet
but the moon is still here and i am looking at you, the most beautiful thing i've ever seen.

oblivion is here all the time now and it is very calm.

coming home was a short walk by the bay and a letter you never answered but as you spell out the sunrise to me under your breath i hardly hear the real of your body or even the confessions that your bones make against each other and this is okay

because the dreamed afternoons are train stations though the train never comes or if it does we do not bother to ride it anywhere except maybe to the next station to sit there awhile and pass the time reading books written with some other audience in mind. it was magic to you that i am still alive but this is a fact i struggle with every day as i seize random clouds to covet in the sky but really just am a thing of aching eyes as the horizon goes and goes and i after, pulling the moon and myself under only to wake in the blue haze of day to sink my own stars, to pull my own gaze and the rotten oars of this little ship as shies away from any shore at all.

you touch my shoulder and now it will ache for months not of you but of all the lost worlds i have left behind and yet continue to live through every day. the wind through these trees still tells of the winter sun does not leave us even for a moment though it ages through train windows, we are glowing the shore. time did not miscount us though. each of us is but one universe and so of course i know your name and have no need to look upon your face but in love as restores this moment before slipping away through the door to wander another empty house shadowed by this endless day as we fall into unbeing, and so resurrect stars.

there was an anything about us

it had been the four of us in the elevator
trying to figure out which brought the stink of alcohol,
trembling the buttons it seemed the second floor
was broken so i got off at the wrong level and found a window
to stare out at the half-snowy rooftop.

the dock leads all the way across the water
we go to the center to look out but there is an immense fog.
a stranger keeps pace with me for three quarters of a mile before i fall
behind or into the water.

i wake up still in a thought of you, as though
the skin of the world was not unbroken and the continuities of
horizon
do not rely on us or the sea. and the broad organ of the sky
were beating a luminous rain of drenching color.

and in the great wound of the earth
there was no suffering except for the kind which you could not
speak.
and in that ache, which was desolate,
you are insurmountable.

we fell asleep at the museum in front of the painting of snow with a white foreground and a white background: knowing you displaced my little skiff far awry, it was your universe eyes. i keep trying to meet you somewhere but i'm afraid you do not know me. i have crossed all the bridges to find the dim fire of through the metal grills the whole city as though it were yours or mine, uncountable lights. only you are somewhere at the bend of that long river into which the sun falls in a dreaming summer stillness where we live as shadow or are pulled formless as lights knowing that we are not landscape.

suspension

from washington's lighthouse protruding to the upper valley, lightless
and small i like to climb the bridges in my bare feet and a body along
the edges and to make it to new jersey only to turn around at god's
small garden, thinking if only

i could show you this most beautiful view of the harbors, the shoals,
the shiveringly wide river in all it is i would but make you love
something as bright and unrenounced as a city

on the lost island, the world all brisk and real again. the scrappy
queens

but this is a blinding wind to lose one in, all there is to do is
remember you, making homes in the dirt and keeping the window
open to the spring night

of brooklyn
through the dead docks and their humans down to screaming neon
of midtown into the sun as it falls

over williamsburg it was a rare infinity

i have been thinking of you and i know that you are sad even though
i do not know you anymore,
not really

stillborn, you
were only the moment that took god's breath away
early this year. no, all through the first hours of that new day
the lord could not breathe. nor could i,
looking at you, caught in the beauteous. but death betook us
not ungently, we fell into this spring storm
after the blue harbors of january, after i broke
silence to tell you how after all i felt
looking upon the realms of your eyes,
rimmed, dull in a senseless ire, the way they beckoned
to old universes and your body was like a wind
for and by no one, it summoned gusts:
something unknown in it. we met in that pale hour
and soon the fabric of the light, the world even
had come undone. but not me, and not you.
it was not snowing there when i wrote you,
the heavens were intact. the moon was mere spitting fire
and the sun, a white shroud enveloped in the snow cloud.
you were shut into the white sky of your beautiful mind
because you were afraid the only thing of you
might not be after all; you cared too much about the world
in your mind is beauteous in all its splendor of wintertime
dreaming. so i go to the wood to bury you, so i find
the imaginary bodies as they lie still and perfect and i
lift them naked into the stars with no brush of
touch to color them, no breath to bury them
as the living did. do i bury our stillborn moment, then?
do i cast the never end? into the sleeping carcass of the earth,
dressed only in snow? did i love you then to tell you
i'd be there for anything only to realize the awful nothing of it,

how when you finally could rest you fell upon my lap like the sweet
child you are
and i cared for you, how i wanted to care for you but could do
nothing so in that early hour i raised your head and left? is this love,
then, an inscrutable burden, like losing the whole universe over and
over?

and upon entering the house, there will be
a ghost at your shoulder with the voice most known to you.
he will tell you that you are magic
but only real thing is the light most luminous held in and out of your
soul
though maybe when you walk towards the lit rooms like a dream of
daylight
you can say that you are scared aloud
to she that will hold you in her drunken stupor and the world will
shudder
until you fall into the corner with the golden child of your thoughts
painting his nails turquoise and lilac and writing letters to god though
he tells you to stop.

he is in a storm of silence again this night
the music is now a whale in its throes and you are glad to be
suffocated by the death of this immense animal a long time ago you
too were cast from the ocean and
summoned into this mortal form and then it was
bloody yearning written into your wrists
a brief history of breath the in and out
and now in memory of a thing called love
but that is not how it happens

instead the girl takes you to the next room where the music is no
longer an animal but instead the whole sea and people, the creatures,
which blindly seek to embrace one another or spin like dizzy stars
through a senseless night and you fight at she has the most brown
eyes. you think you know her from wherever place you wandered
before you were born.

there is a new boy laying on the couch so you hit him. his tongue is plump between his lips you can see the narrows like a riverbed. he is strung out. someone, somewhere is calling his name. they take him to the next room, lay him down, and then carry him out.
your ghost is here with filtered water for the boy but nothing drips through.
you tell him "there is none of your heart in this
it is embarrassing for everyone."

the boy is holding a letter to you and he asks which angel to give it to now that you have died so you rise and go to the sink to drink and the water falls upon your face it sprays and the golden child says you must be born again and he is standing next to his friend who is determinedly destroying an armchair until the tenants of the house rush at him and you take a sip from the cup that is your hands and no one says anything because they are focused on the way you stand

because you ran on the road as the trucks came by you and the sky turned green like a january harbor and you were sunk into a place where no men live but still they stopped to look at you until you returned to the trees that whisper you back into a winter dreaming that universe over there, none of your heart is in it
but in the quiet whereupon you find love and slit it open
seething stars come undone, galaxies all bleeding.
gone is you to give the loss to the ghost so he might know love still there is no consolation for this world.

when you find the ghost again he is quiet and still and smoking a cigarette outside

you put your hands on his face until it is smeared red and you say "so that now you know you are living"
i cannot believe you tried to bite my sullen universe in your bitterest lip
i loved you like oblivion, but
love is losing the whole universe
over and over.

you are inside
central park in snowy listening
to the un-noises: human on mute.
walls are what keeps the out.
you have other worlds in your eyes.
i know planets like that, near where i was born.
looking at you is looking back at earth from outer space.
thank you for you. i am sorry,
for these galaxies.

i am caught in something now
midtown is abandoned and inhospitable,
the homeless curl up against the sides of billboards advertising naked
women
the next morning all is fog an assembly of hijab-clad women
outside columbia, couples talk loudly to each other in the grocery
of future breakfasts
i've made the city to be as sleepy as any other space i inhabit
but otherwise i've found the city to be very talkative because there is
just the always people. the man is eating the wound of the earth his
hands.
i want you to feel okay and also to be near you,
sorry for existing.

born in isolation, i didn't grow up anywhere
but i'm afraid you are familiar.
your beauty preys on me.
i like your gone magic
though i cannot imagine a body known, only angels:
another lake of white under the sky of shrouded light.

the home you are wanting is likely to be this landscape
once it has been rutted in tracks with the pools of light seized
between what is made waste.
leaving is knowing that the ghost of you rises out past anything. your
name no longer means yearning, i am, and of stars. if only there were
something before it was gone. so long, here are your lunar apologies.

after several days of being, the universe caught me where i lay
sleeping and put his hands on my face.

i fell away.

i cannot know but i think you must have terrible dreams of me. the morning was thick with snow but as the sun slipped over the noon, the clouds like pale leviathans fell to higher levels and the light shifted through the sleepy wake until the world was summoned forth into a new era of magic that stretched and lanced shadows, dusk burning off into the midnight pyres of god's thoughts. in repose he wept but knew not what for.

the very next day you offered me the sweetest agonies of the flesh and i said no, the bridges do lead somewhere when we cross them but the new lands are the same. there is only the sky to talk to. there is no blood in you. knowing you is the greatest sadness i have. i am ever in awe of your absence. it means you were here in the first place.

the only great romance to be had is with the earth, moon & stars. so lose me. to know there is something before it was gone. i do not mind you just as the moon does not mind the sun as bares the skin of my back into the neverminds or into existence as the rising light might pretend itself a sky away. a slivered ghost of itself by noon. in that moment of us, we are readied for death.

future objects

always being equipped with a camera that forever fails to capture the light of it, the landscape, the moment, anything or the fact of being alive in places, realizing gradually the contribution of every sensory input and to think, this is not really an amalgamation of perceptions anymore, this is a feeling.

i know there is an imaginary house somewhere upstate for us to live in. yes, i can watch her eat rice plain, colorless as an angel she wanted a taste or even soup after you threaded the sweet scrapped kale through your knife and fed only your heart. maybe in waking she would stretch all the way to the sun across those sheets and then retreat to darkness again. i know all those candles you lit were not made by hand but you went to the market to buy them and also you decided you wanted the smallest room and with no furniture. i know the lights were no gift and that your soul is quiet as you lie awake at night.

blossoms back to under the earth

remembering berlin, of always looking for but never finding the wall
or the landing strip in vienna a crying wind.
schönbrunn was too easy and on the isle of swans couldn't find an
end to the river
prague was a miniature city we didn't know her battles until we
reached the hills,
the homes were forlorn nestled
just as brussels was uninhabitable, buildings with no one in them
and amsterdam was a quiet paradise for anyone on the way to
a london as heavy as the sky on the river.
you and i took a walk in poland, though you didn't know it.
you hadn't been on that continent. i felt your ghost move through me
out past the baltic as though you had been in my heart the whole
time.

when i have died we will be here.
after the train comes, you will think that love can be grown in the dirt

and you will cry afterwards as though it had been
and you had lost. i will go to richmond, baltimore,
and ultimately, new york.

but first i will spend thirty-six minutes in union station
is at this hour, abandoned. i am trapped in a glass shop,
buying kisses and riding the escalator backwards.
i never reach the ground where the train is panting the soft
steam and electric wire, the gridlines take me on to
another place where there is no you.

it is cold on 34th street, he says, asking for a sandwich
what it is like to be fifty-five and homeless,
curled against the billboards and smoking a cigarette.
i wouldn't dream of women either.
i get tired of the isolation of the city, my heart closing over. i hate it. i
hate it. i want to feel the whole universe i want to light something,

i want to love
and to be alone at least to lie on the earth.
i'd rather die in the woods
where the trees still talk to each other and winter
feels like a song or whisper to shut my bones down
as they should be quieted. it turns out, the mountains never care at
all.
i have too many words for strangers, but i'd like to know you

even if it doesn't mean anything when the moon sets and the sun
rises
and the night is wakened as we have been for so long
though our bodies fail to rise like the light in the skies,
i know there is something about us.

what it must be like
to kick in the fence of your ribs,
these that i have watched breathe
and the dim heartbeat like the sun of another world,
like a sleepy home in the earth
or the dim sigh of nightfall as it recedes under
my foot. crumpled, i hope you bleed
red roses, thick, exfoliate in bursts
blossoms in the rabidity of spring.
this night air does us good, it makes you cold
to the world and shaking, i might drown you.
i might have no mercy, because i know you are beautiful. i know what
it means to be beautiful.
beloved, i might as well ruin you. if i really loved you, i wouldn't play
no fish. these oceans tire no one.
i'd have you learn yourself by the light of the moon
and then in the dark, you ought to become a light too.

here it goes. it is true, i have been mad. i have been wretched wild and i cannot tell you the ways i have not been in trouble, but more like ocean trouble as in raising the seas or the turbulence of our times which it is like something we feel in bones and are afraid of without knowing what it is. there is no blood in anyone

but there is a constant weather. it either rains or does not. you only need the landscape for your thoughts. your analysis is a song, you can superimpose your thoughts at any station and where the train goes,

i look forward to my future without a face, the ingenuity of pine trees as they digest my marrow. i am glad that you will not be there. we will be separately buried in the earth. we won't even know it. you will be never and so will i.

i don't support anything except the moon. myself, i am like nothing and to the earth i surrender.

berkshire country
the boy was found in a dumpster,
curled up around his backpack,
just sleeping, not breathing.

he would persist for years afterwards, though he had
drowned his lungs and liver in no little oceans,
an unconscious body hung up to dry, vital signs
like a faint clothesline.

they put him in a room, too.
it was white and he could use the telephone. and after, he might
drive around the town with a hundred bags of easy death.

there is no blood in you anymore.

tuesday, april eleventh/pink moon

a man at the water fountain in central park had kind words for both me and the ghosts he was speaking to. washing his face in it, he told us all that it was a rather nice feeling

to love somebody but it all feels like a spring day i have to count with my fingers because i can't think anymore can't put things together i am in a host of blossoms and always breathless for the universe i have written my will and it says i would like to be made into ashes and even then i will still love all of you and spread somewhere maybe the sea because i might be dying as soon as i can tell about it or worse haunt the living earth a ghost

getting stuck in time again, the rose moon left an imprint you said you were near when looking for a house of dreams, but you are not inside, you are more like an unconscious thought belabored in the light of day, wandering from cherry blossom tree to the horses strung up on chariot in central park looking for a lost way out, a tunnel to stand under when it is not raining

and when the world is less apologetic you go away to hide your head and shed the tears the sky won't give but the blue miracle of sky for which you are sorry, really, you are hoping that death is painful so that your bones know the moment they are cut from feeling rather than being held islands in the riverbed there is nothing for you when it comes to love, just leaving a buried feeling like a moon that hangs crescent its face turned away from the sun to watch all the starry universe come undone

and after this pink moon, i will be glad of you, this universe even as
when i am so nothing.

-

what do you think of planet earth, it only gets weirder subway car shrieking along tracks gathering us all up in its little bursts of momentum before relinquishing, us, like the parrots on lexington not quite flown this is a city of names more than the places to which they have been bestowed still a crowd gathers to view the chorus of them as they land on his shoulder and he looks around grinning until we reach the station where a man sings dylan to us in the resolute silence of those gathered within and without a great city which is only an idea that we had as we coalesced like spit on the pavement dried out by the summer heat or the thick rain will carry us spiraling into that reeking underground or down the distant sound into the sea which is after all only a dream god had when he held his head and felt he couldn't think anymore as we sat on the metal chairs scattered like pigeons in times square, she told me that a man in a blue hat was watching me but my vision is so blurred i could not see though i wanted rather desperately to be alone and have in fact frequented the northern shores along the river and even the smallest toilets in the heights of the city, lately, i've been thinking about the possibility of falling for those we do not know, who are not near.

4.12.17

i know that you live on the -th floor of the building on --nd and
lexington and that your name is v-------- and you go to the ---- school
and you are from a different place. i know your room is painted
purple and that there are many small things on the shelves and you
live across the hall from me. i know you walk like you came here on
your own and there is a soft wind within your bone as though you
had been shaped like a willow, branches blown. i know you have a
radiant face and probably the sun couldn't forget it and that you are
in another place. i am from another place too and try to be not so
long in the city.

escape from the city
i feel like i know you in certain ways but i could be wrong i've always
had this terrible little crush on you but crush more like blossoms
crushed into the hand until it smells like the color of the flower
nothing deliberate you understand

so i took the metro north to your vacated room upstate slept, woke
up in it and wandered the newfound, the air different, clearer, it was
easier to see past love

days and days but i have no tears into the lonesome like and idylls out
here i feel very strange towards everybody i'm not sure that seeing
people is in my blood

don't you think all the ghosts get blown to the waterfront on days like
today i want to stay in the empty house on the spring day,

i'm beginning to think i was made to be alone

i+can%ot+believe+how+easy+it+is+for+people+to+abandon+each+other

the girl beside you on amtrak 244 is draped across the seats like the
swans spiraling upon the surface of the lake in a swoon of summer

on the isle of manhattan there is nothing to escape from or to escape
to
a stifling heat settles by early spring

she says the universe is with you but which one
the spirit of you is soft as light, unrelinquished
the stars have only been talking to you
and you expect a letter but there is no mail

wherever you go, it is very intimate
you are aware that you are falling through someone else's lost time or
maybe your own
will you notice when your grandfather has passed or will you wake
still meaning to visit him years later

this is called a poem.
we took a photo of loss
in the blue room
after dark.

before you were forgotten, you
were many things and you thought you might as well count
though of course you never reach an end, a sum of stars.

i do not want
and i am called light
though i do not see
it anymore.

i want nothing, to pass into me.

your pictures are more vivid than real life
everyone you think you know, your mother and father
they are looking just past your shoulder
as you bathe in the river of your own knowing
wade deep enough to lie on your back
to watch as night gathers thick as summer blossoms
the lightning bugs descend
in the vacant land of desire
there was no one to be found but the ghost of a voiceless boy and
barely you heard the words of him carried on the wind
he says, take my bones
and you give him yours as the earth surrenders itself into you and
you,
into it. you didn't want for anything until the door opened into all the
world of dreaming but now,
the only thing, you say, that will calm you down is being buried alive.

later, you empty your soul from the watering pail in the ease of
midday with no perfect breeze but the thought as holds you out past
the garden

the gospel of saint somebody
i have lost someone but i cannot remember who it was
all that i know is that it is not myself that i have lost,
i am here. someone else is in the borrowed land,
spitting the spirit of the moon in white seafoam
turning the ocean backward until the ghost rises,
and the haunting earth.

you are the descendent of the dead and how i wish you would remember
your own blood before it is gone. but you will not, you are so desperate for a life to live
that you will never find it, breath does you no good,
in you is no color of the world. you are as gone
as the dream of the stars for the universe never did dream,
and if it had, this would be it.

we didn't know each other but we stood in this room
for awhile, stating the same things aloud, in that clouded half-whisper
of blossoms clinging to a nighttime breeze. you put your hands on my face before i knew
that i had one and later i would realize i did not have anything
just as you called my name, not even a name, let alone
a face. there was nothing about us, really all around us,
like a spectre of some great feeling and if i reached up with one finger i might touch
the dome of the silent sky before falling back down to the sea again
to be alone and to know it didn't matter.

by late spring, you have returned to childhood with all the passion

of the sparrows springing into flight, one by one
catching the wind with no thought but the thought of feathers
and the dance of things. i decide that i too am afraid of nothing
and the river is a deeper blue than can be remembered. it is as though
i have given up my bones not to some stranger
but to the unspoken land to which i have always been listening.

they say that everything is softer after we have died
but really, nothing has changed. you speak some names aloud
but there are no bodies to retrieve. no faces to trace
in the angled light of the deep green nights as you once lay awake
within someone's open window until the sunrise shot you through
with terrible fire and you did not resurrect yourself for anything,
not this time. just not this time.

there is no such thing as winter anymore. all you wanted was the
sleep
of my soul enfolded about the primary ribs of your chest. all i wanted
was
to teach the light right out of you, or to pick up your body where it
had fallen
or to lay roses on the space that remained. i wanted to say your name
and i wanted
to see your face, i saw a little universe in you
and there is nothing i can ever do about it.

if humans are creatures of immediacy, then why am i not? is it only the mountainside that makes me feel, and only the night sky to dream. where are you in all this, like a storm over the sea? like dying in one's sleep. or a day clouded by no rain and still the air? it was funny, that time when you thought
you were real.

i sent you flowers from outer space. grown like solitary dreams, like you or me. sadness is like reentering one's body or oneself. in the labyrinth of petals we have no breath, just awe.

i walked right out of my life. and all along the shoreline was a glimmering light as i sank into the sea, or it, into me. i might have been that light but i do not know. i just know it was there, the sun and moon too, its hallowed crescent the only thing that showed what was ocean and what was sky as i floated on my back and deep worlds passed me by. i was not known then and will not be known again. even the stars might have been new to me. i was their littlest aftermath.

i did not surrender to you, i surrendered to the
ancient universe sung into being.

i lost me
in a summer day in and out of color.
my mother, who grew on grandmother's side of the house, says
depression is black and white as my great grandmother
counts her peas she does not
want anyone else to resurrect the disease.
she is a thoughtful, rise early sort of person,
her birthday was a holiday for the children of merida. and she haunts
me like
no one else
suffering from a nausea of the soul
but rather the rafters where the temperature can get extreme. i had
forgotten-
they had books in there too
as his wife banned them from the house. only the bookstore,
which is mystical to the ones who visit from far away the distant
cousins
who really work there.
they tore up the train tracks to make a bike path,
roses blooming in the outdoor bookstore,
there are three levels to the building:
the general store, brimming with books,
the old church, a fire hazard of stacks,
and the elevator shaft, where also is evidence
of a man besotted with manuscripts,
one of the three grouchy old men of cape cod. that is to say,
he was kind
even to tourists always asking for directions to the kennedys'. he was
one
of the last of the muses at the bookshop,

rightly named parnassus.
i am glad that my great grandmother finally met her granddaughter,
years after she was given up by her mother,
out of wedlock and told her the stories of her mother growing up.
it was a personal account written
in that fine hand of hers. they met on the deathbed years before i
came into being. yet i am accustomed to knowing
those to whom my
existence will never be known.

a soul on holiday

there will be pigeons underneath the station.
you will not wonder where i have gone.
the buildings will all be inhabited by a different young people than
they were before
and out on the porches, they
will sway in a springtime clime of cigarettes and wine.

i will have gone to the seaside. the surf also breathes.
a dark cat by the shoreline where the homeless man keeps.
what is it they say? that he sleeps rough?
but no one can see him out there by the rocks
under the cliff alone but for the cat for company,
he builds a little mast and sits astride
before cutting the ceiling in narrow plastic. his house
is a small storm of garbage
out on the lee with a tough meow but at least he knows
better than me in the tide we're all ephemera,
i'm but a missing moon.

discerning the color of your sadness
from afar when i cannot even remember your features,
i might find a knoll somewhere to stand in the summertime
else i might find myself buried underground. without you and me,
the woods here will make their own sound. and it will be beautiful.

when you get tired of this life, i will not be there
to slow down time and pull you out like i did before
when the echoes of the trains all through the valley

was the only waking sound but for the haunting tune
of an omnipotent moon. when the night is soft
and the dove does mourn,
still the ghost knows love alone.

this abyss of sound is a near rain, i am drenched
in the way he was, cold and besotted with wet as he walked
through

were you really quiet then, when you said you had to go
to be alone, did you exist in that fine space
as the sky fell in and the water rushed you
to the cape of the sea, i mean-

did you feel something, do you know what i mean,
a storm of the unconscious as had you, possessed,
did you rave of some sweet thing, did desire

walk the streets in the downpour and the woman with few teeth
asked you, are you lost? you smiled.
is the only space you feel realized nestled beneath
your own brain, like a heavenly glow between your toes
in the morning when you wake to cry alone
and can utter no words but wander the earth desperate
to be rid of all company but the tread of the night air
and the narrow sound of the birds in the bush as they arise
faithless through all the early waking hours.

after rain, the air rises visibly from the streets.
i imagine that we are as one, pronouncing the word
"regardless" over and over until the nightfall,
when the worlds of your mind are realized
in peaceful juxtapose with the city as it lingers
like a grand and complicated ghost
of a thousand dreamed intentions.

i am sorry it happened this way. i am even apologetic for every ounce of my

being here, but i am not afraid. there is something golden about the soul.

acheron
a soft rain of imaginings:
and no easy peace but for the sky as the cumulus float by
and the mourning dove song
like some ancient melody
for which you are hapless, your body mere sound
here i am, gone
as any crying dream of you or anyone,
obscured in the fog so thick
it could be the mind of the trees
or an all-immersive breeze
or the ache of the earth as it comes into being.
i've always dreamt of those i love,
but lately i've had no dreams at all,
not a stirring thought as i bathed
in the river of memory and fate,
just an exhalation of everything
when i reached the ocean and overlooked
the sea of all of it just as it was.

—

iii.

it was strange, seeing you out alone like you finally knew that you were a dream

merely, and irrevocable at that. nothing and no one could make you real.

and still you burned your complete fire,

a distant beacon from which the world was only an ache.

ii.

as the long day closes, and short life comes to its end,

your lies are unmistakable the barest bones of light.

i don't mind you.

i don't mind you at all.

i.

all the love

we have abandoned

it burns at the distant shore:

the first light of sunrise.

aphrodite's orphanage
i took a walk late at night and in the morning woke in parallax
wondering why it was i viewed the world
when i could so easily have forsaken my own backwards tunnel of the
mind
to fall backwards into someone else's.
but then i had that night been
searching for orpheus. but he had no blood
nor even bones and once again
at first light the little bird rose to my breast
singing of acheron so
i went to the river of woe and there
bathed nothing for i was nothing
and lethe tucked me under and i heard that rivers
love each other which is how i reached the sea
but in the undertow i could not remember nor even see
as charon with an animal face leapt at me i told him
i had no money, all i do is steal from duane reade
and wander through the vacant warehouses in queens.
i had kept my mouth closed as the water rushed at me
and there a few words had collected. though my mind had been made
blank i told him a story of a young boy i had known
and thought he might have a universe in him. i said i
liked when people cared about the whole world, though afterwards,
well, grief could not contain the feeling. charon smiled
his sleepiest smile and said this tribute would do,
he drew back the paddles as i stepped on the narrow thing
and we slipped into hades in a gentle spiral
of the steady lee. port authority was waiting there for me
like a song your beloved played once for you

when you were teenagers and you no longer remember what it was like
to hear the first time because all you can remember
are the thousand times in the dark continent that you lay awake
alone with the hope that it would drive you to tears
to play it again but no such feeling reemerged.
you, it seems, were vacant. after a maze of corridors,
you are back on the subway, a man with no legs groaning at you
and the other homeless tucked in piles, occupying
every seat on the car. somewhere, you hear the crying of eurydice
hell was knowing that she had only ever been a shadow.
had the man she wept for been torn apart by beasts, struck by a merciful
bolt or, as charon believed, drowned himself in a thought of her?
i did not know, he was not a man but rather a song.
the city was no great agony but the mind of so many
who, like i, had walked out of my life for a dream.

i fell asleep and the city fell too
into the ground. this was the noise i made with my teeth and it was
the sun.
love was a child that i sent away
it was better that

she sleep rough like the bundles in the new york city.
she kiss only open air and stars be real.
otherwise, why make it out alive
as another organism with its own mind and own thoughtless tongue
ruined myself over and over in the inexplicable and
inescapable sadness of my body,
as just by existing, i was absent.
and on the day when i ran away and saw you at the bottom of the
lake
it was a miracle because it was an infinite fall into your basement
where you curled around me, we might've been
dead children too.

we had killed her many times
but still she had the sweetest smile

because universe passes universe in the unwatched night
when once we slept wrapped by the blankets of another mind
oblivion was sweet but you did not learn
the most beautiful thing, irrevocable,
had been gone from the start.

in a song of stars through universes i fell.

i asked you to come to the parking lot to watch me fall, but i did not want
to not be forgotten
to have a person who might remember
me, in that simple storm of color and sound that was real life.
stepped out of the real life,
i could hear my aunt as though in the next room the cadence of her
unmistakable as a sparrow-walk through the summer undergrowth or
dull splashing of a depressed mother in the bath
or the engine running in the car as i leaned out. what is it like to
know someone
or something beyond oneself. it wasn't like that time last fall when i
flew to the spirit
realm amid a host of ghosts hardly disguised as autumn leaves. this
time there are so many bridges on the way overlooking miniature
cities that i have lost count
of you and the snow that was barely melting yesterday i spun on ice
and turned hapless into the blossoms
as seemed to erupt from every surface. i know you had wanted to
touch me to see if you could be real
and touch somebody. but these phantoms only slip through each
other: to inhabit the ache of the earth,
one must truly haunt, and own something of that haunting. i lie like
the barest bones of light,
i cannot even feel the existence that is myself
which is really ruining because there is no otherwise to undo the
mourning song of one's own. all i know is the most unfathomable
love.

another district
on the day you could speak love aloud, a metro train
filled only with youngsters outfitted
in hard hats without stopping, passed
through the station. you could hardly bear to say it
even then. i circle monuments,
a storm of gnats above the reflecting pool
as the sunset bathes lincoln sitting
so large. this city is in a glow and i am alone
in the quietude of the real.

there is no city except a city in fog before anyone. had woken as the trees moved in an otherworldly breeze. there is no ocean but the ocean. before anyone was stranded on a distant shore overlooking the bluffs of crazy sorrow. and here is the horizon that first finds the sun and moon as they rise and no stars but these stars as cannot be traced. by anyone. i saw you in a dream but then it was only seeing you in a dream. when still the ghost of you walks this earth. we are made of and for all there is is loss.

we made the moon solid in our thinking as we moved
through gaps in the underground
broken between cold stone molars
the city was not asphyxiation
though inside a billion tiny rooms
and lives piped like sunk stars,
this was only a certain kind of endless dreaming.

and in existing, i am happy that you.

though it is so hard, like staying all night on the pier without thinking
under the stars

and not moving before the ghost moves

and the voicemail i have not yet deleted

as though to record a night and play it back,

hoping it means the same thing each time

though now we have followed the path back into town

where it becomes more difficult under the sun we must move
ourselves

through the daily hallucinations and out into the next world

i cannot forget some things like the rise and fall of your heart now
that is gone.

that is each moment i have been dreaming of the dead

as though they might dream of me too. as though love were real and
nothing new.

the verse

there's a suffering that will overcome you, when this happens there is no ending it. you will make breakfast & sit out on the veranda

to hear the birds. your heart's small universe will fragment or implode. it is your job to continue living.

you are like the sun that rises without a thought over the whole world. you cannot even think of the moon.

to whom you dream a little light of undying love. this too will destroy you.

no july
i was on the trail (and there were power lines like the time she told
me there were power lines and like that day listening to changes in
the rain on the highway where the truck almost hit

me before i met the boy wearing a crown of sorrow and the bluest
eyes dripping like the dense green after the storm which never came
only a white thunder in the sky like being alone but for the thoughts
constructed like great spare tents filled with the sound of the radio or
articles in the times)

as opposed to being in a place.

all my dreams died earlier than usual this year. children's faces pressed against the glass as the wipers duck and rage against an ensuing storm. i didn't go to the southside or to any side of the city i just sat on the ground as close as i could to the river and i looked as far around the corner of the shoreline to see no one looking back at me. i guess that yes, it is easier to love someone through an infinite sum of happenings in the world surrounding you rather than if they were around but still i'd like to crush the unknowns between my palm like the petals near the sound. you can really smell it.

i wish there were things to believe in like rowing a boat along the copper river round the crest of the land and naming it after a president before placing a breadth of stone that is when i say i miss you it means the whole wide world though i too am a universe and forgotten in the thick. i came here to write this poem but i don't know if i'll ever come out of the haze of my mind as it dawns and the fog burns off like the haze of his mind as it burns you might say i am tired of being okay but only because i have all this love to give.

you stretch a world in your mind until it breaks, fragmented, the glass flowers of existence in your bare hands bloodied, are you still sitting under that bridge are you still counting the heartbeats for the dead, don't be afraid, nothing is forgotten, we are all mud in the morass, and if you enter the woods there is always the the great the soul the somber tone,
the no reason.

dear you, i feel awful strange saying this but i was just thinking of that moment when we found the pale white ships floating through a harbor of sound and every motion was broadcast into a dream from then on as i fell backward it came over me like a ghost or like a great albatross i was in the shadow of. i liked looking into your eyes though they needed so much they needed nothing at all i tried to tell you that but it didn't work clear. did the ocean ever come so near as it did then i am not sure of even the sky which you held so near your chest i remember how you'd shudder late at night from the oppressive weight of it the whole world i mean.

and dear you, i am sorry that i woke out of that night like i did knowing some truth about you that you never meant to tell but this is the consequence of falling asleep over a stranger after exchanging a few words in the predawn you must understand i came with no harm to give but the woe of not knowing you, not knowing you at all and still dreaming the sweet fog as burns off over the city.

and you i don't so much want to speak to any longer the grief that you are is not mine but still i would hold the ache if it would make you feel, if you could love something beyond yourself.

i have spoken to the dead and they say that in the end there is a marvelous world. and when walking through the tunnel, open your eyes and the dark will turn green as the trees until you reach the chapel at the end the chapel that you have not remembered until now, and when you wake from this world,

do you wake into the sea or what do you wake into and is there some truer thing to say than i miss you

i was hoping you might hear the tremor of your own thoughts in the nighttime as you reached to pull stars from the morass but no luck we reversed the car out of the lake and out of the wood and swung round far past the moon as it illumined the silent ache of the earth and all that has ever come into being.

you are bare bones in the morning and a dream of the night. you know the whole earth but you wouldn't wish it on anyone.

what is it they say, that there is no ending anguish? has anyone ever said, there is no end to grief. when you find something outside of yourself, there is no end. i am sorry for the earth and the stars too.

i see you are forgotten in this thick and terrible mind of july. i see you are in the heat going. this means we could be any nonsense. it is not dark as it once was but still the house is there in the broken field and someone might just have the radio on upstairs. you're not coming back but neither am i. if we are both away, then what does the land look like? it looks like solace but it also looks like the whole universe as the stars come on one by one in mourning. this vestigial sadness won't do. it's like a young bird on your desk in the upstairs room and sometimes you stretch its twigged wings with your hands. you say the thing will fly. sometimes you are home and sometimes not. the light stays on. i forgot to tell you this anecdote when you were falling asleep but most of the things i say are better said now that you have passed on. so i will write it down like a letter to the ground. i was walking one day in the wintertime in search of a place to end my life. but once it was over i knew i would fall limitlessly through myself so it would never quite end. i found that the sunset had me turning back and i answered only to myself when i walked i found a ghost house and i crept about its entrances like a curious mind. i opened the front door and you were not there. i walked the stairs and again, you. i entered the upstairs room and the light was on and no you. there was no bird on the desk. there was no radio playing the blues. there was no me and there was no you. i sat for awhile then so my soul might catch up with me and when it finally did, the whole universe flew in on a pair of wretched broken wings, a flock of ravens muttering in the backyard. i walked out the door knowing that no one would ever live in the house but the ruin would perpetuate as long as the silent revolutions of the moon. there was a shrieking chorus of crows nesting in my hair and myself, i was utterly bare. the light shone out from the window onto a scarred front lawn. in its glow you stood calling out and i was left wondering how the ghost of you had followed me from an empty house. you were crying desolate, pale and frantic, like an hour for which there is no answer as i walked. there was nothing i could do. i heard only the nightbird song. to this day i cannot hear your name or see your face. i cannot remember a line or curve of you. your soul is the whole world so there is no discerning it. in late summer i am nothing but the mourning dove.

i went to the hills you know (i came from the hills) when you said it is lonesome out there but no one really cares, i know what you mean. i know what you mean and i know what you mean. i understand most of all the curvature. where it goes no one can tell but it is there and the telephone wires are tucked about in every shaved woodland of this continent and i could send a pulse down one i really could or out into the radiating air i can even imagine (the whole world) as the fog heat rises from the pavements in the aftermath of all that is summer or the aftermath of living alone for so long and never anything else before just dying as the sun dies every day but then returns or the moon which we speak of only in wanting though it too tilts the earth and it too. and when you said, it is lonesome out there, i said no it is full of the world and yet, yes one can be alone on the summer day beneath a summer sky, yes, one might be gloriously alone. especially when a mind is sunk like the pools about the quarry stone which is in the heart of gold and the heart of this world.

palisades

i may not remember you but then this may not be the last snow of
the year.

the stone saint who overlooks the bluffs melts a tear.

it is an misnomer that we ever

encounter anyone else beyond ourselves.

it is all about the nuance, a grey february sky or a flock of nothing
birds. i might just live

for the illusion.

please forgive me for my foraging in your backyard for pockets of light: i confess i get uneasy in the night wind, lying on my back watching the leaves shudder headlights. from afar, i see my parked car as the man beams a flashlight looking for, what, lost lovers, a hot box, there is none. the grass of the baseball field is uncut. the moon was made to be held in both hands even as she slips away. it's okay i'll miss you as long as it's raining. the sleepy child of the gentle mourning merely blessing her own little head as tears fell into the wading pool that is the world beneath, still unknown, still yet unbaptised in a dawn aglow.

this is a eulogy to my shadow as it is bitten by the dark as i am taken yes to another world where nobody dreams strewn galaxies and other vacancies.

i don't know where it is, life. i tried to keep the window open to hear the cicadas chirping but midway through the night i had closed it with my feet. i called up a magic boy on the telephone and he said you have so much to say and i said i haven't spoken in days and the line went dead, breathing was too easy. they haven't fixed the canal yet. the riverbed is cracked dry in the heat. being sad was a gift because you got to care about something in the first place. i watch the water glasses collect beside the bed as though in a movie the observed habits of the protagonist but there's no story and nothing here is even ugly it goes from full to empty, i mimic the passage of time. i guess i don't know when you are here and when you are not it makes no difference the universe moves in and out of vision you said, i hate it when you talk about the world that way and i tried to find the fog of the morning as it burned off and as i, too, disappeared like a cloud taken in the sun and wind as if i too were the illusion here as if i too were not something made of shadows buried to get out of the summer heat. but this is not for you, this spectral wandering along the haunted river has no end really and the sea really, and the sea to be alone but for the sea.

that night, alone again crossing state lines on foot in the cracked mud of the canal between sirens, foraging owls, drunken crowds and homeless
watching them live lives through a vacant buried mind, this heat of dead july
after no light of midday and no real person walking the streets but this who moves through myself, a ghost? isn't the universe emptied yet,

you sit inside to eat ice cream during the downpour. everything's getting so personal. you'll cry over an impersonation, you'll cry over her. there was only one person you could bear to be around but that was before you knew the colour of their fear. i do not know why there are people outside or why there is daylight as i am very slowly leaving my life, i wish i knew someone who would sit in the same room and not say any words.

when the morning fog clears off, opens a whole mind of sky. life without you is easy but there are less dreams intact like souls wandering off a breeze above the water, sometimes i wish you were here and could see it only so that all the awe of this world could move through your body.
to be honest, it was really just a dream.

eight track

how strange to be as real as the ridgeline of mountain meet sky and to hear the sound of you breaking my heart its colossal ruin of the ice sheets in late february the organism of river cracking its innumerable vertebrate and to be glad of it

sweet to hear the cicadas singing us into a haze of summer while the crickets foretell autumn though seasons are always in the past now that we have grown older and sadder and forgotten some love to the fading leaves and stranger trees

to have imagined your own shadow as you walked and to be struck in awe by any merest glimpse of another to name it wonder and hardly ever not think of it after though all comes to this dust of my tongue and me, buried in a dream like that spring that had me so shut away

felt the glow of my own soul again, enough to light up the world, but only the love that brings us back again through this thick infinity,

i do not think i have yet forgotten this world.

claremont

you become intractable, in an informational haze in the woods you sit
without seeing no desire consumes you you cannot rise
you don't want to see anyone but you are bored and when you invite
them, they come and you are bored or merely alone in that you
answer to no one but your patterns are tiresome this is no cabin in
the wilderness or even a place to bathe naked, this is the nakedness
itself like a fly on the back like the permutations of railroad tracks
your spine. he comes out for you to ogle his bare body and you are
careless you want nothing more than to be away when he looks at
you you see nothing new in this universe has already happened

real im not real the dust of your heart of your life of your mouth
coming and going and being alive
the temperament of the world was neutral. you said you could hold a
bee in your hand. and not be stung? and maybe not be stung. look, at
what nature created! us, and everything else.

poem unopened

You come back to the world you were in before as if you had not
lived other roles in the other worlds waking in each room as if your
body had been painted in before the dawn and the soft contours of
the flesh were not illuminated but made of light itself. Perception is
all in your undoing. Late at night, the owls shift and hum and we step
over vacant spaces. There are no foxes. The dog you were supposed
to care for hides his head and growls when you come near. You hold
out a bowl of stillwater- he snaps and dives. You confuse his growl
with passing trucks but listen again, making sure he is still there, okay
and alive. You step away into other worlds and other things as the
books beside your bed pile up and the lamp is on or off in the
daylight you say you want to go away. You sit on a stoop and watch
the other kids play fighting with used milk cartons strapped to their
wrists. Every boy and girl you meet wants to embrace you so you
stand farther in a prayer. Like a kind comment or humor that dries
up in the well and the water is now piped from town but sometimes
comes out of the tap white. You tried to go back into the woods
when yourself you had felt ill but the sky was bare and the birds were
crying warning and many things were moving about mysteriously so
you rose quiet to make away in a mess of omens none of which you
owned. You have been followed by foxes or no foxes. Rabid or
grinning. Barking young male foxes, circling and crying out for
something. You have no desires. You want to lead them on or away
but mostly back into themselves into the brains without saliva. You
cannot make out the number of tails or souls in the animals and you
do not understand mythos. You feel wanted like never before. Every
night it is waiting at the end of the road that you once nearly drove
off of into the ravine past the danger road closed signs but you never
did and the creek is forested gently and leads nowhere trickling.

Every night you walk past the creature. You head towards the ghosts in your house knowing that they are busy with their own lives and won't bother you so long as the back staircase is left open for them after dark so they can watch television in the basement undisturbed. And so long as the bathtub upstairs is unused they may bathe themselves and lay naked upon the porcelain surface. You leave the outside light on for any stray spirits after you go to bed.

29th

my demons are in that part of the wood
where it gets darker earlier than the rest of livingston.
i was supposed to be caring for them creatures you left in my house
have the walk of the place like the mold growing on the couch
but i didn't. a relief to have nothing to say here
only hello as we pass by. i don't want you
because how beautiful you are like being real
without me which is not where i plan to live.
it's all about how you encounter the crow
or whether you can take the end of the world
like melatonin and a glass of water lukewarm.

most mornings i go to the old estate to talk to the ghosts. we haven't spoken since last september. i want to give up your ghost. you don't have to watch me do it. the animals dwell in pockets of the wind and as the spirits pass the crows cry out in dirges. we are nested, ravaged and preying on one another through the steeped sunlit passages of the next world which is this world which is.

on the day john ashbery died, it was slight and raining
which confirmed that the universe was as it should be,
we all knew it, could feel it
like the magic of a mind and spirit of the natural wooded world
and condensation which is the breath of all of anything
and he was in that thick somewhere breathing still
i could feel on the neck of the earth that is us
i turned in the bathroom mirroring myself, convictions layered in the
blue
irises only to be held up to this, or anything else
as soon as i put the words to paper they meant little more
than what i could find of love in the attic room

lyme

a day in the grass and i come upon a disease in my skeleton.

joints undone, there is a question, i say- am i losing my mind as in suffering i seem to suffer

from nothing. but a weakened face. they said existence is your only headache

and my thoughts are made light upon the surface,

in pain, of the earth. but there is no doubt in my mind as the rash spreads

i have no breath, only a small storm on my forearm: blacklegged, tickbite

delivers in my blood *borrelia*
burgdorferi. from which comes
the fever of me. three weeks-
it was late, do you feel this heart?-
i feel intravenous
brimming with antibiotics,
doxycycline, amoxicillin, or *cefuroxime axetil.*
overcome, i am post,
even as the bacterium life is extinguished,
a fire in my tissue, the body as ember
burnt out.

after,
am i here or have i become a symptom of my skin,
here is an epoch of new sleeplessness,
of new tiredness, and the way the memory goes
with no way to digest this head of pain
i move, i twitch, muscles thrown in paroxysm

through the nowhere lands i have less of a thought in me
as though an impossible depression. my bones worn,
in a fatigue i walk the landscape. is this the aftermath of a ruined
kingdom .
of my own webbed tissue, or the unknown storm that still gathers
in me, the secret colonization of my flesh, the bacteria still alight,
resurrected as i fall? there is a great uncertainty
about my heart.

Do you know how the seasons change lately, they change and are not lately, anything. Today is autumn, grey-skied, the wind rising us up and carrying us out, somewhere. I am a hooded figure with a German Shepherd on a chain leash and I walk on the side of the road picking purple meadow flowers and playing Schnittke. Maybe you know something about this, but I doubt it. The doors all close and open of their own accord and I have a thousand empty rooms in an old farmhouse to myself. Someone took me out to the bar last night but I don't care. I was going to live a life but I've retired. I need to get out of my room but there's nowhere to go and suddenly it's colder than it has been in weeks. I feel like throwing up but I haven't the energy. You want to know my energy, or passion? It's at the laundromat but I won't walk there across the bridge which is broken unless I find the cat who slept in my bed with the guest who was uninvited. It is all so perpetually boring that we often create false patterns to struggle over like fault lines shuddering the mountains against each other on a planet, abandoned. I miss the exam. You don't know my name and I can't remember it either. You will soon stop talking to me once you realize that there is no mystery and the obscurity of my mind which you think you can see upon my face is in fact, nothing. There is nothing to be figured out here. There is no puzzle and no conclusion. There is just a memory of being in the past and an attic where we left love in the bath. It doesn't matter if the house is haunted, we are all living here anyway and we can call it whatever we like.

what aches

of extremities are laid out like winter trees shivering in a nonexistent
breeze,
blood has an end to it. i could watch where it runs frantic
but i do not mind and tend these aches like the premature child
that i am this is only a skeleton of thoughts
no longer color but an in-utterable light that is the fluctuation of your
ribs when there is so little air in them and a heart that slows like the
soft feeling of the moonrise just over the hill which was once dark in
a way that was like no other darkness that we might remember but
that does not make it so
i am tired, everlastingly. a vacant sun today and the sky just
a vast haze. i would take you to my heart but that is in the hinterland
that i am
not blessed or cursed to roam any longer. i cry for elizaville, and
milan, yes,
and the lake of the deli which is god the surrealist's fond memory.
i have lost my sound, the crows flung out like dusk
and the waterfalls now pooling only in my veins
underneath the skin, unbruised and perfect. this is ruin,
to be unloving, to be taken out of suffering,
to be a fool giving nothing to the world. this is
deepest surrender.

i could read you something i found in me but then again i could not.
i feel like the february that stills the water.
or like the silence that glows out from every harbor along the river.
maybe it is pain to be built. like a nothing tree
to be riddled and free, ready to be taken by the wind, i have no end
and i cannot bear to see you either.

corrosive, kitchen faucet sadness

like a dead cat but the cat isn't sad anymore because it's dead so it's
just the observer who thinks it's sad that the cat is dead only i think i
might be the cat, which is dead there is something you cannot handle
but that is a different story and not related to the dead cat
you should've said hello
i could read you something i found in me but then again i could not.
i feel like the february that stills the water.
or like the silence that glows out from every harbor along the river.
maybe it is pain to be built. like a nothing tree
to be riddled and free, ready to be taken by the wind, i have no end
and i cannot bear to see you either.

contrition

death is what is framing your ankles, the collar, and the bone of your face

i wish i could hold your body through the dark but i have nothing in me

i have forgotten myself and sit in this world only to pass the time

i wish the peace between ourselves could illume this vast and empty world

to make things better for you and anyone even if there is no sound in my soul

(sad-tiredness:
that feeling of like i want you to feel ok)
regarding this (and care for you through all time and space) and
regarding, and regarding this-
nothing "left to the imagination", all comes true as the maine
summers picking real cognizance through the blueberry bush
(which as you go dissolves into a dim delusional but irrepressible
private tragedy)
undreaming, unburdened & breathing
a death that talks to you on the same side of the hour,
something else that ruins you after. something as sweet
as you. get to be inconsolable in your white house alone as the wind,
you get to be inexplicable as
in the bathtub upstairs, there is nobody there (and an inescapable
feeling of). there is nobody there and there is no one, soft.
do you want to know- what it means (loss)-
i am glad that you are here to read this.

you propose to me
as if you and i were anyone saying
october is unseasonable. bye, i love you over the telephone.
tell me the story again but this time
wear the other jacket. this woman who made my heart
tells me i am polluting my mind with all this nothing
and i tell her to tend to her skin as it flakes
petals off a fruit, which, bruised and overripe, fall
senselessly everywhere she goes, she is lost again in the corridor
and i have found the room beyond this world
which has no color in it but the miracle of existence
which is the only house we have to live in
until we are ready to no longer
pass the time like cornfields in your car upstate in the autumn
which is no autumn for me because the only autumn was last autumn
when i found
where the crows would take
my body and the sky was burial
it was no small thing there
i don't think you've ever been alone like that, no one has been alone
like that
as much as immortality or finding your shadow and pulling it apart
remember when you came to find me in your green car or was it
sienna
as i stood in a stranger's yard or in the fire station or with my thumb
out into the road, hoping taconic
that there was surrender out there somewhere and it was real and true
in the time that it has taken to write this, i have realized-
my heart still is beating.

it is very cold out here and i might tell you that but it means very little because
there is no other feeling:
you can find a lot of things at a yard sale
i once found the dearest person to me whom then i lost
as many times as the rain falls
again and again on any given day
and another and another,
a few silly things that i buried myself in
and consequently raised a host of sorrows
which never quite vanished on the wind-
who like an old man speaks soft
through the ridges. i can only dream that one day
the wind will be me.

why do you look for me
what is this in you that makes me
so sorry. if kissing is a lot of information all at once,
thank god i never have
anything to say to anyone.
are you always this way and yes, you are always this way and so, and
so-
the river which is no river
beside the train tracks that might take someone past the horizon and
into the sky-
this hudson makes me oh, tired

new jersey fog insular the intersections hanging wires and glowing
stoplights as you take me from one rest stop to another (your
constant refrain of abandonment

in a crater laughing through an archaic beginning of the world sort of
darkness while i have faith
the fucking men on horses galloping through philly in october street
lamp
because she has particular eyes, something nearly green blue,
fathomless kind and important-
wild you, looking out
what are you afraid of
what am i afraid of? not doing my best for you
wasting myself in ways unlike this winter sky
in its crustacean solace, clouds split
cold as cowrie shells.
i like
to sit with this pain
or a long impossible plane
time folds
there is something out there that is not you
so you surrender to it too
in the western hills it greys to feel
flesh sinking back into
a dim miracle that i still have these bones
this is last time we will all see each other

im glad she loves you or,
im glad you love him
that's the last place i saw her
statue glowing white in a wood
i hope you too can see the world
maybe more of it than me-
it will all go on even when i'm gone.

without this world i would have even more nothing in me
inside of the meaning of love or outside of it

a foregone
there is nothing on the curb of wisconsin avenue
or on the potomac where among the homeless
pressing my face against the asphalt
as if i might torture the landscape
into something that meant something
the hills taconic that were like falling in and out of love every evening
as it got darker
and the cold was easy,
deep as the burial ground was rich, had i known death before
inside the firehouse, meaningless
you asked to borrow a phone so she would come get you
in the car that could have been red
but it is no longer

i wrote you that i could someday love you
so i never saw you after the first morning
at seven cold beautiful light that was not blue or green
as we looked out from your window
just another beginning of the world.
you were asleep when i said your name
and a dead animal
i was the only one in the january building
as i took my own life through the bath
where you will find all the traces of what came before, so haunt your
own house
if you lay back into this- an ocean of- forgive me- you might find that
there is very little left to do here

animals were always running out of the house

he and i searched for that dog
in the eleven woods
trespassed on the lands
without a chain leash
in through the echoes of partygoers
as they walked on the highway without turning
cars from behind.
one day you will get very tired.

would you take me up, my dear friend
and put my bones back?
before george washington and key and brooklyn and the other
there were so many bridges

i am just now finding aspect of my memory coming in like the light at
odd hours
in the winter. had i taken a life then?-
you get to be the ghost that you give up.
it's alright then
you can lose it all now.

i have been in some ways
no one knows how to talk to me
and i don't know how to be anyway
so what does it matter
whos going to see us out here
whos going to close our eyes when we die
whos going to take our bones to the river
whos going to know us and hold us through the green hours of the
morning
whos going to pull us out of the snow when we fall asleep in the cold
dont we all have mothers and fathers that made us
arent we miracles only here to pass some time
why can't we make good of it
passing the time is losing those few things that one had the
opportunity to care about in the first place
or passing the time is caring about a few things in the first place or to
pass the time,
you might say to your friend as she drives you through the fields of
autumn that you are here
to "pass the time"- it is strange to have known you for one very
infinite moment
and then never again. if in the dream you were real
what are you now? if you are here, you will always be in some ways
terrible
there is no house and no boy inside of it
all that's left is im so glad you all exist.

5:38
came into this world
took a picture of loss
can i go now

dead men like to talk about
the smell of the sky and your sad ocean eyes
sitting and thinking
like i wish i was
so alone that the land couldn't trace me
and i could take the body out
and i could free the stars behind me
but i had no wake

except this sound
nothing i give anyone "works out"
why don't you play your brick wall harmonics
into the ground thank god there is no grace in your fall
i've buried my illusion
it is my face
waiting for my veins to pop skin like my mother's and her mother's
this poem's no good
after death the memories of you slowly leave the skulls of your family
and friends
this is why i hope they give me no mound
id rather be by the ocean taken up
or the silly ashes

id rather have this moment if you don't mind
i know i can't keep it

if you were to be on the hill, or if you were to see-
there is a ghost ship moored not far from here-
it is tethered by a strand of wind,
weighted by the dawn of the world,
which is tomorrow. maybe i will see you there
and all the ones i knew before
though no time could keep us there,
hours still somewhere in your heart
which, like a strange unlikely realm
lingers on in the dry
winter. the world does not thaw
just for you-
we are not moved by any particular breeze
there is a light on just beyond these naked trees
do not name it mine, do not name it yours
as it comes on and then goes

december 1
it is quiet now and i dont want the sound of the thought i said aloud
to travel up and down the river, disturbing those in the midst of deep
vast dreams of their own

moon-worship

wearing someone else's coat i emerge broad shouldered

the man with the new dog walks the block

he says my two girls are "like a chorus"

how he came to the end of street

now that you are stuck with the other creatures of the planet

choose ones that leave you lonesome in the right places

the house is no longer haunted but there is energy in the sheets and
the curtains and the corners of the

objects contain sleeping ghosts

it is best now not to talk to them

crustaceans in the sky

dodging the wild inconsistencies of linear time

inhabiting one place or another

no moral respite or the sigh that extends your breath

we better walk down to the fucking river

past the railroad tracks from which we fled

from the water which was looking for us

piped and illuminated by its own sound

like the brain subterranean, is this fog dense

as you go out to your parked car in the moonlight

"to get something" or to look at that bright

lady, lunar, impassive satellite

and if she were to say a word would you swear then also

that you were just projecting thoughts again into outer

space. it is like when someone-

though not that unlikely dark neighbor-

is staring at the back of your head and you notice

or like the sad obliviating realities

of being loved.

train 290

still on wisconsin ave in the 95 daylight

after the part of the morning which was late at night

snowdrifts and emptier spaces

fear fresh and newfound

or the dull syllables of the grey lakes of winter

whom do you mourn for

it's not open to the public sweetheart

post no bills

someone is drinking your bathwater

the moon is watching

you in your parked car

another few thousand

wilmington or in other terms, no place
between a built home of false monuments
and the cacophonies
as though the mutterings of us all
were not rats
chewing through the discarded
sounds in subway tunnels.

it is funny that after you moved into the house by the river the
neighbor's black eyes have followed you not merely within the
confines of that house but also everywhere else as though this
disembodied thing were meant to follow you ever after
though you explain you are of no particular hauntings
and in being a ghost there are not so many things to do

this is a very busy train
in which humanity was ugly or it wasn't
in which you have no blood
this is the wrong part of the story because there was never any music
except for yours which is gone and this being the case, there is no
concept of the real
and there is no real, and afterwards
we spent our lives in a funny little twilight of the world

it is unlikely that you will be here
for no purposes but the purposes of being
these being, frankly overwhelming as well as incredibly
dull as though life
was fixating on anything
as though

at some point in your narrative, you reach the porch which is empty with
one light on and one light flickering. and nothing is easy and
everything makes sense,
even this scene was not in its heart constructed

today it is winter and winter and then still winter and after, winter
to inhabit
to be real on the outside
to be senseless and strange and possessed by no thought
or to nightly, breathe back the incantations of the moon
or to write this just as the secretary
of some foreign entity who dictates language
and does not fill it in at all. perhaps the dancer
as though spacing
were as specific as love, which when inattentive,
is so often damning.

are you ready for the beginning of the world, it is coming so soon
no one will be there except you and your beautiful animals and a
distant relative of heartbreak, that is to say the stars, of someone dear
to you who you cannot see in waking life but nightly they dream of
lifting you out of the snow and dressing you in warm clothes.

in the winter do not move drink hot water be a well intentioned ghost
and stand outside in the cold
have you felt anything lately through those thick warm walls that
somebody else built
yearnings are so easily given into nothing
the moon i cut into my wrist one day in april is gone now

the feeling i had for you once
was another small universe
there are so many people like possibilities unmet
the sheets were not folded over the bed
the room was full of dolls and he smiled when i left
there were chocolates from portugal
after i left my own journeys behind me
in the snow, a punctured tire

i don't know that i am writing this
but i recall the wall was just barely
too high
how are you too much, i'd like to know
and like humans we tried to
climb it or walk through the scattered pools
where the sky got trapped
between the trees talking about
texas beach or belle isle
which is my sweet

if there were squatters in the old nail factory,
they would build fires to keep warm
as the ghosts walk the wall

and the door at the end of the world stays open

the february ice has not formed yet
over the river, wait until dawn gathers at the rim of the world
all day long even as darkness stretches later and later
you will be so bleak, you will come into something
like i saw you and knew you at once without having met you
which is an aphorism for love
as though that is what keeps the universe together
and us strangers

in this particular
walk through the woods
in the waking quiet
snow, after sun
fell past the shadows which could
be trees or shadows
the cold is felt,
and also to be at the end, nearing something
as though one could be near anything
except the thoughts
which move you through the preternatural
frost is like magic
and you are like no one
which is soft and even wise
in conjunction with how the planets sway
and name nothing or how you come upon
the eve of the world as it sinks away
thinking to yourself
if death is like forgiveness
love is surrender
to an outside that you do not know or see.

i have been to the end of the world so often
enamored with desolation isolation whites greys cold early darkness
and the way light is at the rim of the sky, dying only seems bad from
inside,
with no heartbeat i don't know why

i walked down to the train tracks in the winter cracked and there by
the river the bodies floated down like some stygian metaphor never
to be dressed in warm clothes again my memories would not stick or
sink lethe had me in its midst in icy torment i went on to the old
place, my bones burning senseless ire, as like shards of light the souls
left

there is such a thing as a place after all
even after watching the souls float down the river on that day in
february
thank you for letting me find you in that which makes you so tired
that you would
dig your own grave
and also for this moment though i know we cannot keep it
of there being something beyond oneself, that is
and caring
or to give, something, and the stars were very clear in the lavender
dark which was like no other dark.
i suppose we always know the story from the beginning and i
suppose it is different having lived it
death was not so much like nothing
just beyond the barest imagining
the vocabulary of this world and that world and the other world
maybe
to translate nothing
is not unbearable
to see you, yes, that is what it means
you are distinctly unbearable
you are riveting and sleepless and kind
i'd discard the word sweet here i think,
what is one universe to another

make up a dream to tell me when i next see you.
i was glad to. give you. what is it- a place in this time of mine that
does not pass
the pulse as comes down from your mind your skull i felt against
mine
you are sweet it is terrible
you contain- so much information-
i will unbury you as best i can
i would take you to the river if i could
to resurrect every strange nothing
i am glad your soul is here
even when it is not,
there is something in you.

the sleep of knowing

is a sleep of another

there is no real lullaby to your thoughts

though there is an uncanny stillness of being

i would like to deconstruct you, yes-

in a manner of days

to "think you through"

or to breathe you real

though this too, is unnecessary

was that obscure living room, necessary

did it keep you well?

i hope, and it kept you well

the soft light which is dark and hallowed at most

and livid even,

which is at its heart, so quiet.

she is your mother
she, was like the most people in a house
on summit drive in western massachusetts,
not north but the town over
and she didn't mind nothing,
and i wanted to do something kind for her
as kind as she was to me,
waving goodbye in the garage
saying i love you to each of us as i took
her daughter back
to school in new york,
even if just turning the television off. i said i love you too,
her muscles would daily weaken which to us living was degeneration
but to her was like a way out, blossoming into a place that we do not
yet understand
like springtime when it is still winter here in our hearts. soon we too
will thaw, will fall, will flower into the dirt and no burial
will take us out of the earth.

adams to annandale
memory is quickly fractured and so it becomes necessary to gather

parts remaining like icicles held cold and reddening the bare hands

to spend a day or hour is disbelief or swimming in the frozen river
looking for the things i once knew

small on the trees and small also on the air with the phone lines in
gusts in the small and deep held along the tracks and houses and
roads but mostly small as a thought in my mind

to turn the corner, as in evening snow the earth turns blue

i always find myself on this stretch of road, a bend in the cornfield and white empty farmhouse thinking i know finally, where i am, that i am either just learning to pass the time with my mother, no less, or that i may call you sweet or her sweet or him, sweet which some say is mutual understanding and others say dismissive though snow accumulates with that same ease of acknowledgement standing round and finally looking at each other we are not, sometimes i send you a few words of how i feel about you and other times we pass by each other thinking we finally understand this stretch of road.

i wish i knew you well enough to be quiet with you but you are not sure about walking in the snow to get here only to walk back again even as i show you my new cat i am a strange person to know and i'd like to know you if that is, good for you

the snow meant that a white light hung about the house, every window subdued by the pearlescent glow; i was leaving soon and above the mountains the heavens were broken into another color which could not be described.

Taconic State Parkway

One might find the landscape itself at least dramatic except that it is all the same. The road was intended for the landscape, but the hills are ubiquitous, and so the landscape is of mostly nothing.

The parkway is actually less eerie in the fog (because it decreases the distances) and not at all like its cousin in the Shenandoah which is as soothing as a lullaby in those blue hills. It is empty enough to be cited in art history textbooks, empty enough also for Aunt Diane to kill seven children in a car crash. It is easy perhaps to go the wrong way or even to go crazy on the parkway because the lanes are apart from one another. Rather than decreasing the distance between passenger and wilderness, the separation of the lanes in this way only emphasizes the isolation of the human body in a landscape. Its gentle turns are suitable for a commuter traffic that never appears. Through the inescapable experience of asphalt, man makes himself foreigner here and for no reason but a tremendous lack of feeling which is called the Taconic State Parkway which is a road that traverses Westchester, Putnam, Dutchess, and Columbia counties and is all much the same. I'm happy to say I've been lost here and here and here, but only for a little while.

consolate

how is your night
strange i don't think it's mine
i began to think for the first time yesterday
though in not being here it is rather hard to see
you were calling my name i think in your mind- i could hear it,
you could not hear anything such was your repetition like
there is a secret choir in the earliest spring
it is quiet because it is wild
and so is not meant to convince anyone of its sound
and afterwards the snow
which is a harsh erasure-
enough to make the oldest of us unaccustomed to living
as if to be attentive, or to spend prolonged periods of time.
ice floes are where
the organism is broken
it was a river.
for this or anything,
there is never any consolation.
i am not her, but rather what comes after, to be
after her which is no syllable and i wish
in the first way that wishes were born
like snowdrops or lily of the valley,
as if moon and earth could be wed but really
they may be looking at each other-
so all suffering, or you might call it love,
was for something after all.